IRELAND

Big Buddy Books

An Imprint of Abdo Publishing
www.abdopublishing.com

Julie Murray

www.abdopublishing.com

Published by Abdo Publishing, a division of ABDO, PO Box 398166, Minneapolis, Minnesota 55439.
Copyright © 2015 by Abdo Consulting Group, Inc. International copyrights reserved in all countries. No part
of this book may be reproduced in any form without written permission from the publisher. Big Buddy Books™
is a trademark and logo of Abdo Publishing.

Printed in the United States of America, North Mankato, Minnesota.
032014
092014

THIS BOOK CONTAINS
RECYCLED MATERIALS

Cover Photo: Shutterstock.
Interior Photos: ASSOCIATED PRESS (pp. 15, 16, 17, 19, 31), Getty Images (p. 29), Glow Images (pp. 11, 13,
    25, 27, 35), iStockphoto (pp. 5, 35), John Shearer/Invision/AP (p. 33), Shutterstock (pp. 9, 11, 19, 21, 23,
    25, 27, 34, 35, 37, 38).

Coordinating Series Editor: Rochelle Baltzer
Editor: Sarah Tieck
Contributing Editors: Megan M. Gunderson, Marcia Zappa
Graphic Design: Adam Craven

Country population and area figures taken from the CIA World Factbook.

Library of Congress Cataloging-in-Publication Data

Murray, Julie, 1969-
  Ireland / Julie Murray.
      pages cm. -- (Explore the countries)
  ISBN 978-1-62403-343-8
1. Ireland--Juvenile literature. 2. Ireland--Social life and customs--Juvenile literature. I. Title.
  DA906.M875 2014
  941.7--dc23
                                    2013046917

IRELAND

CONTENTS

AROUND THE WORLD

Our world has many countries. Each country has beautiful land. It has its own rich history. Its people have their own languages and ways of life.

Ireland is a country in Europe. What do you know about it? Let's learn more about this place and its story!

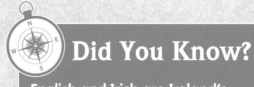

Did You Know?

English and Irish are Ireland's official languages.

Ireland is known for its green land.

Passport to Ireland

Ireland is in western Europe. It borders water and one other country.

Ireland's total area is 27,133 square miles (70,273 sq km). About 4.8 million people live there.

WHERE IN THE WORLD?

IMPORTANT CITIES

Dublin is Ireland's **capital** and largest city. About 528,000 people live there. The River Liffey flows through the city.

Dublin is filled with historic buildings. It is home to a busy airport and ports. The city's products include cloth, electronics, and food and drinks.

Did You Know?

Dublin got its name from the River Liffey's dark water. *Dubh linn* means "black pool" in Irish.

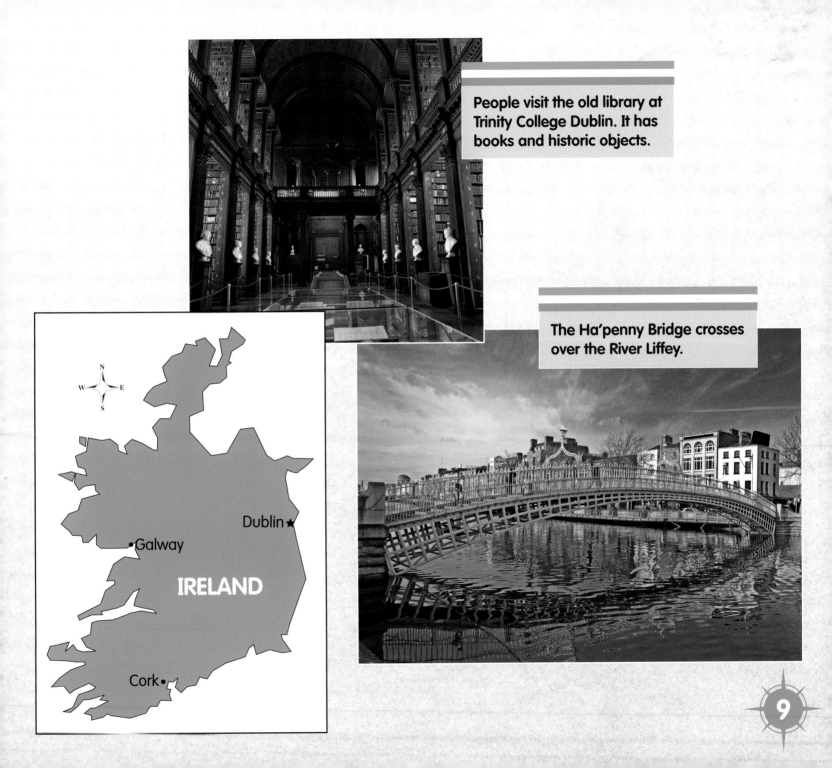

People visit the old library at Trinity College Dublin. It has books and historic objects.

The Ha'penny Bridge crosses over the River Liffey.

IRELAND

Dublin ★

•Galway

Cork•

Cork is Ireland's second-largest city. It has nearly 120,000 people. Part of the city is on an island in the River Lee. Food, steel, and cloth are made in Cork.

Galway is Ireland's third-largest city. About 76,000 people live there. It is on the west coast near the Atlantic Ocean. The city is popular with visitors.

Quay Street is a famous area of Galway. There are pubs, cafés, and shops.

Cork is known for its beautiful churches.

Ireland in History

People have lived in what is now Ireland for thousands of years. The earliest people came from Europe's mainland. They lived along rivers and hunted and fished. Over time, settlers built homes and stone monuments.

Around 400 BC, **Celtic** tribes settled the land. They brought their own ideas and ways of living. The Irish language began with these people.

The Book of Kells was made by Celtic monks. It is famous for its art.

Over time, other groups controlled Ireland. In the 1500s, the United Kingdom (UK) took power. In 1801, Ireland became part of the UK.

The Irish people struggled for independence. They wanted freedom of religion. And, they wanted to make their own laws.

In 1920, Ireland split into two parts. Northern Ireland stayed part of the UK. In 1949, the rest of Ireland became the Republic of Ireland.

When Ireland became a republic in 1949, people filled the streets to celebrate.

15

TIMELINE

Around 432

Saint Patrick arrived in Ireland to teach people about Christianity.

1592

Trinity College Dublin was started. It is Ireland's oldest university.

1845

The Irish Potato Famine began. Ireland's potato crop died. About 1 million people died from hunger. Millions more left the country.

1949

The Republic of Ireland began on April 18. At that time, Ireland was among the poorest countries in Europe.

2012

Boxer Katie Taylor won an Olympic gold medal. This was the country's first in 16 years!

1916

The Easter Rising took place in Dublin. Irish **rebels** fought for freedom from the UK. Nearly 500 people were killed.

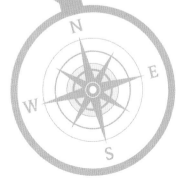

An Important Symbol

Ireland's flag was first used in 1848. It has three stripes. Green stands for Roman **Catholics**. Orange stands for **Protestants**. White is for the hope of peace between them.

Ireland's government is a **republic**. The president is the head of state. There is also a prime minister. The Parliament makes the country's laws.

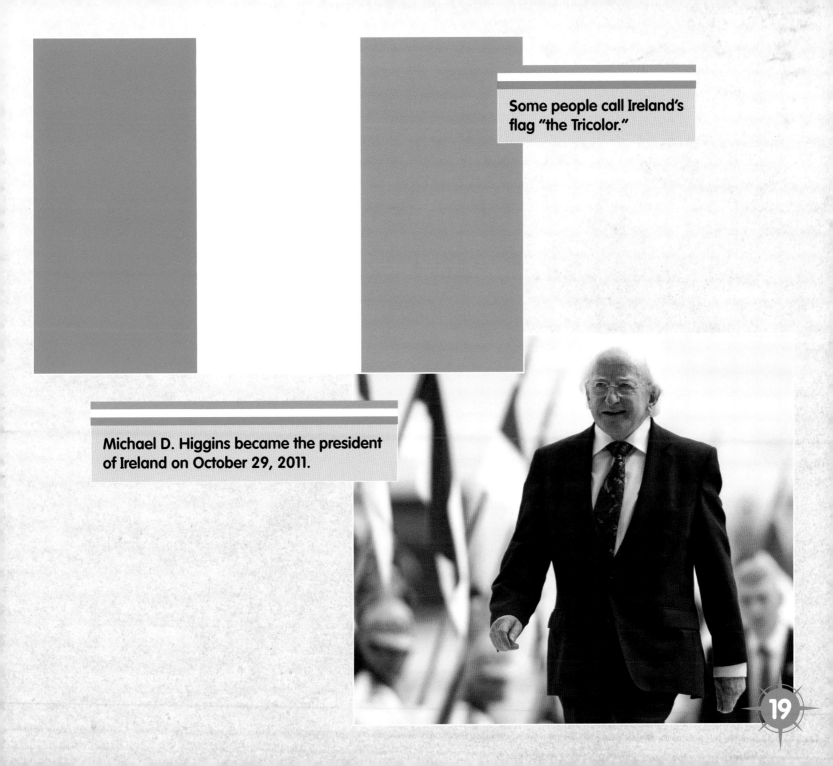

Some people call Ireland's flag "the Tricolor."

Michael D. Higgins became the president of Ireland on October 29, 2011.

ACROSS THE LAND

Ireland has gently rolling farmland. There are also wetlands and forests.

Mountains and rocky cliffs rise along the coasts. Carrauntoohil is the country's highest peak. It rises 3,414 feet (1,041 m).

The River Shannon is Ireland's longest river. The Lakes of Killarney are known for their beauty.

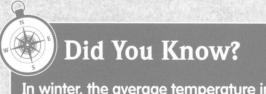

Did You Know?

In winter, the average temperature in Ireland is 41°F (5°C). In summer, it is 59°F (15°C).

Ireland has rock walls that are hundreds of years old. People built them by hand.

Ireland's animals include deer, hedgehogs, otters, bats, and badgers. There are no native wild snakes. But, there are more than 400 types of birds.

Ireland is covered in green fields. It is home to some forests. But, the land is mostly covered in grass and moss.

Wildflowers bloom in the mountains in southeast Ireland.

Deer and other animals live in national parks.

Earning a Living

Ireland's factories make computers, cars, and cloth. They also make beer and whiskey. People have jobs in banking, education, and health care. And, many serve the country's visitors.

Ireland has important **natural resources**. It is a leading producer of lead and zinc. Crab and lobster come from its seas. Farmers grow barley, wheat, and potatoes. They raise cattle, chickens, and sheep.

Sheep dot Ireland's countryside.

Waterford is famous for its crystal. It has been made since 1783.

LIFE IN IRELAND

Ireland is known for its beauty and history. People travel there to see castles and the countryside. They visit cities to go to plays and museums.

Traditional Irish foods are simple and hearty. They include potatoes, soda bread, Irish stew, and shepherd's pie.

Did You Know?

In Ireland, children must attend school from ages 6 to 15.

The Temple Bar is one of Dublin's famous old pubs. People go to pubs for food, music, and fun.

Irish step dancers keep their arms and upper bodies stiff.

The Irish enjoy horse riding and horse races. They also watch and play soccer, Gaelic football, hurling, and other games.

Religion is important in Ireland. Most people are **Catholic**. Some are **Protestant**. Many belong to the Church of Ireland.

The Irish Grand National is a famous
horse race. It is held every year in Dublin.

Famous Faces

James Joyce was a talented writer. He was born on February 2, 1882, in Dublin.

Joyce was known for trying new styles of writing. In one style, he ignored sentence structure. He wrote down ideas and thoughts as they came.

Joyce died in 1941. His poems and writing remain popular today.

One of Joyce's most famous works is *A Portrait of the Artist as a Young Man.*

Bono is a singer from Dublin. He was born Paul Hewson on May 10, 1960. Bono is the lead singer of the rock band U2.

U2 began in 1976. By the 1980s, it was popular worldwide. The band is known for its strong sound and style. Hit songs include "Sunday Bloody Sunday" and "With or Without You."

U2 includes Larry Mullen Jr., The Edge, Bono, and Adam Clayton (*left to right*).

Tour Book

Imagine traveling to Ireland! Here are some places you could go and things you could do.

**Remember**

Kilmainham Gaol is a famous jail in Dublin. People go there to learn about Ireland's fight for independence.

See

Visit the Cliffs of Moher in western Ireland. You might have seen them in *The Princess Bride* and *Harry Potter and the Half-Blood Prince*.

Ride

Visit the Ring of Kerry. It is a 112-mile (180-km) driving route in southwest Ireland. You'll see old churches, a castle, and other beautiful sights.

Smooch

Kiss the Blarney Stone at Blarney Castle near Cork. It's supposed to be good luck!

Explore

Connemara National Park is known for its rolling hills and mountains. People go there to hike near the lakes.

A Great Country

The story of Ireland is important to our world. Ireland was formed by strong people who fought for independence. It is a land of green hills and historic castles.

Ireland's people and places offer something special. They make the world a more beautiful, interesting place.

Kylemore Abbey is a popular castle to visit in western Ireland.

IRELAND UP CLOSE

Official Name: Éire (Ireland)

Flag:

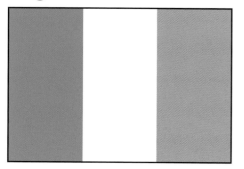

Population (rank): 4,832,765
(July 2014 est.)
(123rd most-populated country)

Total Area (rank): 27,133 square miles
(120th largest country)

Capital: Dublin

Official Languages: English, Irish

Currency: Euro

Form of Government: Republic

National Anthem: "The Soldier's Song"

Important Words

capital a city where government leaders meet.

Catholic a member of the Roman Catholic Church. This kind of Christianity has been around since the first century and is led by the pope.

Celtic (KEHL-tihk) relating to people who lived about 2,000 years ago in many countries of western Europe.

natural resources useful and valued supplies from nature.

Protestant a Christian who does not belong to the Catholic Church.

rebel a person who resists authority.

republic a government in which the people choose the leader.

Websites

To learn more about Explore the Countries, visit **booklinks.abdopublishing.com**. These links are routinely monitored and updated to provide the most current information available.

INDEX